Police
HORSES

by Sunita Apte

Consultant: Mary Hamilton
Certified American Riding Association Instructor
Riders Elite Academy, Inc.

PUBLISHING

New York, New York

Credits

Cover and Title Page, © Luis Santana/Xtreme Xposure Photography; 4, © Tristan Hawke/ PhotoStockFile/Alamy; 5, © Luis Santana/Xtreme Xposure Photography; 6, © Bettmann/CORBIS; 7, © Courtesy Library of Congress Prints and Photographs Division; 8, © Museum of the City of New York/Byron Collection/Getty Images/Newscom.com; 9, © Bettmann/CORBIS; 10, © AP Images/Marty Lederhandler; 11, © Liz Hafalia, San Francisco Chronicle; 12, © George Bridges/KRT/ Newscom.com; 13, © Tom Carter/911 Pictures; 14, © Geoff Howe Photography; 15, © Geoff Howe Photography; 16, © Geoff Howe Photography; 17, © Chang W. Lee, The New York Times/Redux; 18, © AP Images/Tracy Deer, The Connecticut Post; 19, © Luis Santana/Xtreme Xposure Photography; 20, © Daniel Valdez; 21, © Daniel Valdez; 22, © Stefan Rousseau/Topham/PA/The Image Works; 23, © Anne de Haas; 24, © Andrea Mohin, The New York Times/Redux; 25, © Luis Santana/Xtreme Xposure Photography; 26, © Bonifacio Pontonio/Absolut Vision Stock Vision; 27, © AP Images/ Eugene Hoshiko; 28, © Liz Hafalia, San Francisco Chronicle; 29TL, © Bob Langrish; 29TR, © Bob Langrish; 29M, © Ralph Reinhold/Animals Animals Earth Scenes; 29BL, © Bob Langrish; 29BR, © Robert Maier/Animals Animals Earth Scenes.

Publisher: Kenn Goin
Project Editor: Lisa Wiseman
Creative Director: Spencer Brinker
Photo Researcher: Amy Dunleavy
Design: Stacey May

Library of Congress Cataloging-in-Publication Data

Apte, Sunita.
  Police horses / by Sunita Apte.
    p. cm. — (Horse power)
  Includes bibliographical references and index.
  ISBN-13: 978-1-59716-401-6 (library binding)
  ISBN-10: 1-59716-401-1 (library binding)
  1. Police horses—Juvenile literature. 2. Mounted police—Juvenile literature. I. Title. II. Series:
Horse power (Series)

  HV7957.A68 2007
  636.1—dc22
                    2006030439

For more information, write to Bearport Publishing Company, Inc., 101 Fifth Avenue, Suite 6R, New York, New York 10003. Printed in the United States of America.

10 9 8 7 6 5 4 3 2 1

Contents

Caught

The robber grabbed the money from the frightened bank teller. The **heist** was going just as planned. Now all he had to do was make a quick getaway.

When he stepped out into the bright Florida sunlight, however, something large blocked his path. What was it? The robber gasped as he looked up. Officer Dave McGrath and his horse, Dirty Harry, stood in his way.

Like Officer McGrath, police officers all over the country patrol cities on horseback. This officer and his partner are keeping the streets of Dade City, Florida, safe.

A police horse and his rider can stand over ten feet (3 m) tall. They are sometimes called ten-foot (3-m) cops.

Terrified, the robber ran back into the bank. He dropped his gun and the money. Then he put up his hands to **surrender**. He knew he couldn't escape from a policeman on a horse!

Some horses wear badges so that people know they are part of a police force.

A Long History

Horses have been used in police work for hundreds of years. Long before there were police cars, officers often traveled their **beat** on horseback. In the mid-1800s, sheriffs, marshals, and deputies **patrolled** America's Old West on these animals. They often had to cover great distances between towns and farms. They could do this quickly and easily on a horse.

A deputy in Arizona in 1886

Soon towns grew into large cities with lots of people. These areas needed more than one officer on horseback to stop crime and to keep the peace. So **mounted police units** were formed. These groups were modeled on the **cavalry**, a successful army horse unit.

A mounted cavalry

Police horses are sometimes called four-legged cops.

The First Mounted Unit

In 1871, New York City became the first place in the United States to have a mounted police unit. This group had 12 policemen and 15 horses. From the beginning, New York's police horses were a big success at stopping crime.

Other cities took notice. Two years later San Francisco also created a mounted police unit. Soon, almost every large city in the country had police horses.

Mounted police officers during a parade in 1897 in New York City

In its first year, New York City's mounted police unit made 429 arrests.

However, less than 60 years later, things began to change. In the 1930s, the use of police cars became more common. Some cities decided they didn't need as many horses anymore. Many reduced their number of mounted units. Others got rid of their horses altogether.

As the use of cars became more common, police departments began to rely on horses less and less.

Keeping the Peace

Crowd control is a mounted police unit's most important job. Officers on horses watch over groups of people during **strikes, rallies,** and parades.

Mounted police officers help calm this crowd of angry protestors in New York City.

In crowd control, one horse can handle a job that usually takes ten police officers working on foot.

While on the job, these brave animals have helped save lives. During a protest in San Francisco, a crowd got out of control and surrounded a group of police officers. Sergeant Phil Downs knew just what to do. He had his horse lead the other officers right through the crowd. The trapped officers escaped by following the path the horse had cleared.

Mounted police are also great at patrolling wilderness areas. Sitting high on a horse allows an officer to see far into the distance. A horse can also move quickly through forests or long, narrow park paths.

Sergeant Downs patrols Golden Gate Park with his horse, JR.

The Best Breeds

Almost any type of horse can be used for police work. Common **breeds** include Thoroughbreds, Quarter Horses, Percherons, Clydesdales, and Tennessee Walking Horses.

Horses need to be brave in order to deal with crowds.

Police work requires a good, **obedient** personality. **Skittish**, fearful, or **stubborn** horses that don't follow orders won't do well. Strength and size are very important, too. Horses need to be strong to walk on patrol all day. Also, people are more likely to obey someone riding a big, powerful horse.

Some horses have had other careers before becoming part of a mounted unit. Many police horses were once rodeo or show horses.

Many mounted units want their horses to look alike. So they mostly use dark-colored animals with few white markings.

The Finest

To find the best horses, most mounted units use the help of special ranches. At these places, horses begin their police work training.

At the McClelland's ranch, horses are thoroughly trained before being sold to police departments.

Some mounted police units want their horses to be age six or older. They think young horses are not **mature** enough to handle the work.

Scott McClelland and his family own one of these ranches. They are very careful about the animals they choose to train. They look for ones that have a willingness to learn and are well behaved. They also make sure the animals are alert, strong, and healthy.

The McClellands look at many horses. For every 100 horses they see, they may accept only two into their program.

Scott McClelland grooms one of his horses.

Training

Once a horse has been chosen for police work, his special training begins. The animal must learn to stay calm in crowds. He needs to be comfortable on noisy streets, surrounded by cars.

Each ranch uses different training methods. For example, at McClelland's ranch, a horse walks through hanging plastic strips. The animal can't see through them. He must learn to trust that the rider knows the path is safe. This trust will be important for the officer's and horse's safety if they ever have to control a **riot**.

Scott McClelland teaching a horse how to trust his rider

In big, noisy cities like New York, well-trained horses are very important. Before they start working, New York's police horses are put through an additional training course. They learn how to ride through fire and how to behave if a gun goes off near them.

A trainer helps some New York City police horses get used to loud noises by hitting a wooden stick against a metal pail. The animals' training lasts for three to six months.

Only a third of the horses that enter New York's training program make it into the city's mounted unit.

Building a Bond

The relationship between police horses and their partners is very important. In most mounted units, police officers work with the same horse every day. During their time together, they develop a good working relationship that is based on trust and affection.

Officer Edgar Perez grooms his partner, J.J., before going out on patrol in Bridgeport, Connecticut.

Mounted police officers are usually responsible for caring for their horses. Each morning, the officers report to the stables. There they **groom**, feed, and saddle the animals. Throughout their **shifts**, the officers take frequent breaks to give their four-legged partners hay, oats, grass, and water. Taking care of their horses is one way that the officers and animals build **bonds**.

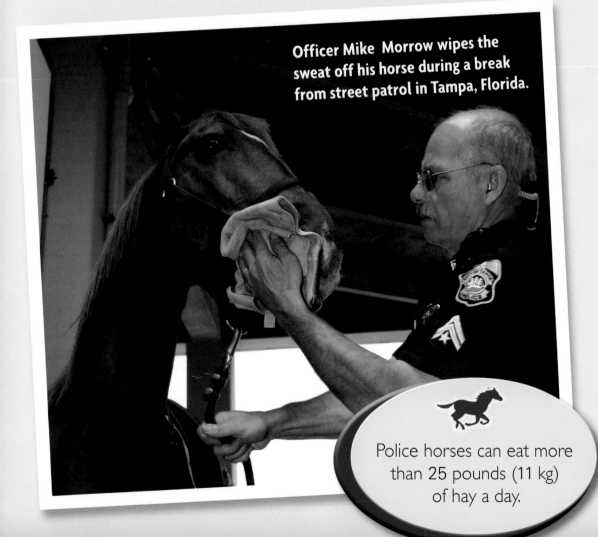

Officer Mike Morrow wipes the sweat off his horse during a break from street patrol in Tampa, Florida.

Police horses can eat more than 25 pounds (11 kg) of hay a day.

Best Friends

New York City police sergeant William McKay and his horse, Angus, have been partners for nine years. At first, they mainly helped control crowds in parks and during parades. Recently, however, their job has changed.

Now, Sergeant McKay and Angus patrol one of the city's highest-crime neighborhoods. Riding high on a horse helps Sergeant McKay stay safe and spot trouble. He has a great view of everything that is going on.

Sergeant McKay and Angus

Angus also gives Sergeant McKay added power. Most people don't want to start trouble with a police horse. As Sergeant McKay says, "When a cop on horseback issues a **command**, people tend to listen."

People who might be shy around a police officer will often approach a horse. This helps Sergeant McKay easily build friendships with people in the neighborhood.

Hard Workers

The job of an officer and his horse is not easy. People or other animals may attack and injure them.

During riots, police horses have been punched and hit. Sometimes people throw things at them. In 2002, Alamein, a police horse in London, England, was trying to help calm down an angry crowd. Someone threw something at him and seriously hurt his leg. Twenty-five other police horses were also hurt. Fortunately, they all recovered.

Alamein and Sergeant Alistair Blamire, after the horse's recovery

In most states, it is a crime to hurt or injure a police horse.

Sadly, police horses can be killed while on **duty**. Brigadier, a Canadian police horse, was hit by a car during a routine patrol in 2006. He died at the scene. Officer Kevin Bradfield, who was riding the horse, broke his ribs and hurt his neck, back, and legs.

Brigadier's story touched the hearts of people in Canada and the United States.

Life After Police Work

Once they become too old to work, police horses get to **retire**. Each community's police department decides where their retired horses will spend the rest of their lives.

A retired police horse farm in upstate New York

Horses usually live for around 20 to 25 years. However, most police horses retire during their late teenage years.

Some police horses are sent to farms where they are allowed to roam freely in **pastures**. Other retired animals find new homes with volunteer families. These farms and homes are inspected to make sure the horses are well cared for, fed, and groomed.

Mounted police officers often visit their retired horses. The bond between officers and their four-legged partners can last forever.

Many police officers remain good friends with their retired four-legged partners.

A Growing Trend

History has begun to repeat itself. As they did in the late 1800s, mounted units are once again springing up. Police departments everywhere are realizing the value of the 10-foot (3-m) cop. There are more than 85 mounted police units in the United States and over 30 more worldwide. Countries such as India, Australia, Hungary, Finland, and Israel all have mounted police units.

Italian military police and their four-legged partners in Rome

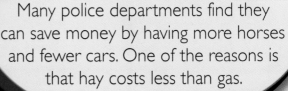

Many police departments find they can save money by having more horses and fewer cars. One of the reasons is that hay costs less than gas.

These numbers aren't surprising. In areas where there are mounted police, crime tends to go down. It's no wonder these strong, brave heroes are being welcomed back onto police forces around the world.

Mounted female police officers on patrol in Dalian, China

Just the Facts

- Horses, like humans, need to be careful in the sun. In 2006, a heat wave in London gave Sunny, a police horse, a very bad sunburn. A drugstore donated five gallons (19 l) of sunscreen to protect him.

- Most police horses wear horseshoes. However, some mounted police units have begun using **unshod** horses. Many riders think these animals are healthier and make better workers.

- Mounted police units have different ways of naming their horses. One unit in England names them after the towns they patrol. Some New York City police horses are named after officers killed on the job.

- Police horses are tough. In 2003, a San Francisco police horse, AAA Andy, was chased and bitten twice by a pit bull. Andy's injuries were very bad. However, just weeks later, Andy and his partner captured a **burglar** who had committed more than 60 robberies.

AAA Andy

Common Breeds

Police Horses

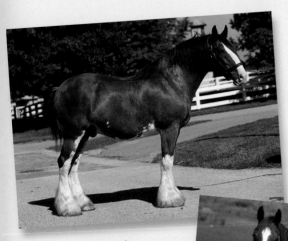

Clydesdale

Percheron

Quarter Horse

Tennessee Walking Horse

Thoroughbred

29

Glossary

beat (BEET) the area or neighborhood a police officer patrols

bonds (BONDZ) close connections or friendships

breeds (BREEDZ) types of horses

burglar (BURG-lur) a robber; someone who breaks into a house or building to steal things

cavalry (KAV-uhl-ree) a group of soldiers on horseback

command (kuh-MAND) instruction given to be obeyed; an order

duty (DOO-tee) the work required by one's job

groom (GROOM) to wash, comb, and care for an animal

heist (HIGHST) a robbery

mature (mah-CHUR) experienced, able to make good decisions and act in a responsible way

mounted police units (MOUNT-id puh-LEESS YOO-nits) groups of police officers and the horses they ride

obedient (oh-BEE-dee-uhnt) when people or animals do what they are told to do

pastures (PASS-churz) grazing land for animals

patrolled (pah-TROHLD) traveled over an area keeping an eye out for trouble

rallies (RAL-eez) large groups of people coming together to offer support or help for a person or a cause

retire (ri-TIRE-yur) to stop working, usually because of age

riot (RYE-uht) an out-of-control crowd of angry people

shifts (SHIFTS) set periods of time in which a person works

skittish (SKIT-ish) easily startled or frightened

strikes (STRIKES) events in which people refuse to work because of disagreements with employers over money or working conditions

stubborn (STUHB-urn) not willing to give in

surrender (sur-REN-dur) to give up

unshod (uhn-SHAWD) without shoes

Bibliography

The New York Times

news.bbc.co.uk/1/hi/england/humber/5149090.stm

**www.ctv.ca/servlet/ArticleNews/story/CTVNews/20060307/
police_horse_060307/20060307?hub=TorontoHome**

Read More

Green, Michael. *Mounted Police.* Mankato, MN: Capstone Press (1998).

Mattern, Joanne. *Mounted Police: Working Together.* New York: PowerKids Press (2002).

Learn More Online

To learn more about police horses, visit
www.bearportpublishing.com/HorsePower

Index

About the Author

Sunita Apte lives in Brooklyn, New York, with fellow writer Michael Sandler and their two children, Laszlo and Asha. She used to ride horses as a child and has always loved them.

37